POETRY ESCAPE

POEMS FROM SOUTH CENTRAL ENGLAND

Edited By Debbie Killingworth

First published in Great Britain in 2019 by:

YoungWriters
Est. 1991

Young Writers
Remus House
Coltsfoot Drive
Peterborough
PE2 9BF
Telephone: 01733 890066
Website: www.youngwriters.co.uk

Book Design by Ashley Janson

SB ISBN 978-1-78988-200-1
Printed and bound in the UK by BookPrintingUK
Website: www.bookprintinguk.com
YB0393Q

FOREWORD

Since 1991 our aim here at Young Writers has been to encourage creativity in children and young adults and to inspire a love of the written word. Each competition is tailored to the relevant age group, hopefully giving each student the inspiration and incentive to create their own piece of creative writing, whether it's a poem or a short story. We truly believe that seeing their work in print gives students a sense of achievement and pride.

For our latest competition Poetry Escape, we challenged secondary school students to free their creativity and escape the maze of their minds using poetic techniques as their tools of navigation. They had several pathways to choose from, with each one offering either a specific theme or a writing constraint. Alternatively they could forge their own route, because there's no such thing as a dead end where imagination is concerned.

The result is an inspiring anthology full of ideas, hopes, fears and imagination, proving that creativity really does offer escape, in whatever form you need it.

We encourage young writers to express themselves and address topics that matter to them, which sometimes means exploring sensitive or difficult topics. If you have been affected by any issues raised in this book, details on where to find help can be found at: **www.youngwriters.co.uk/support.**

CONTENTS

Independent Entries

Hilton D 1

Dame Alice Owen's School, Potters Bar

Lauren Lisk (13) 2
Simran Misir (12) 4
Natalie Kuper (14) 5

Priory Hospital School High Wycombe, High Wycombe

G C (15) 6
S H (16) 7
Blake J (15) 8

Putteridge High School, Luton

Kemi Soyele (12) 9
Ami Catherine Giles (12) 10
Alessia Clapa (13) 11
Saphia Murray (11) 12
Gracie Eve Coomber (11) 13
Isabelle Johansson-Ward (11) 14
Ayaan Uddin (14) 15
Sophie Browne (14) 16
Ben O'Hara (12) 17
Madison-May Lena Orchard (11) 18
Ellie May Worboys (12) 19
Eryn Phillips-Westcott (13) 20
Harvey Daniels (12) 21
Libby Bennett (11) 22
Rebecca Gibson (11) 23
Aryan Reid (12) 24
Isabella Cowell (12) 25
Jojo Moloney (11) 26
Adel Leona Toth (12) 27
Shreeya Radia (12) 28
Jamie Thomas Croot (13) 29
Alex Gibson (13) 30
Daniel Adewale Akinyemi (11) 31
Steven James Wilson (14) 32
Jake Breheny (11) 33
April Brown (13) 34
Serena Mepani (14) 35
Adam Tirletti (12) 36
Chloe Angel Remorin (12) 37
Leo Howard Geoffrey Scott (11) 38
Katie Behrens (12) 39
Kate Starkey (12) 40
James David Armour (14) 41
Scarlet Samantha Louise O'Dell (12) 42
Riyana Mepani (11) 43
Bethel Obuseh (12) 44
Luke Joshua Whiting (12) 45
Joe Field (12) 46
Peter Schneider (12) 47
Daisy Brown (11) 48
Mia Dehnert (12) 49
Nasra Daoud (12) 50
Tegan Sarah Jo Ridey (13) 51
Liam Stoll (13) 52
Ela Yilmazgul (11) 53
Libbie Conquest (11) 54
Oliver Johnson (13) 55
Joshua Bush (11) 56
Asfia Khan (14) 57
Lewis Pedder (13) 58
Harvey Ben Taylor (11) 59

Queenswood School, Brookmans Park

Sophia Mikou (13) 60
Taylor Tao (17) 62
Lisa Okrah (11) 63
Sophia Evans (12) 64
Darcy Evangeline Cheesman (11) 65
Amber Smith (13) 66

Royal Latin School, Buckingham

Evie Simons (12) 67
Lara May Evans (11) 68
Kerensa Telford-Johns (11) 70
Finn McGarr (11) 71
Freyja Barker (12) 72
Jaskiran Munde (11) 73
Chloe Elkins (11) 74
Olivia Aggreh (12) 75

Sibford Senior School, Sibford Ferris

Henry Macer (12) 76
Maia Luxton (13) 78
Margot Connop (14) 80

Space Studio Banbury, Banbury

Kelly Lloyd (16) 81

St Margaret's School, Bushey

Eilidh Colla (12) 82
Beanie Bond-Ryde (12) 85
Lauren Crush (12) 86
Roma Mehta (12) 88
Sherlene Olayinka (13) 90
Lybah Aleem Ahmad (12) 92
Varsha Mahendran (13) 94
Amarleen Brar (12) 96
Emer Brownleader (12) 98

St Thomas More Catholic School, Bedford

Kate Maynard 100
Satasha Angelica Kumari (12) 102
Sandra Kulovic (12) 104
Autumn Clare Theakstone (12) 106
Temiloluwa Ajao 107
Aimee Williams 108
Elliot Tempest (11) 109
Justin Lau 110
Selina Borrelli 111
Marco Catania 112
Keira Stringer 113
Ciara Delaney 114
Naveen Prem 115

The Cherwell School, Oxford

Natasha Lancaster (13) 116
Rita Iannacci (12) 118
Leah Niamh Marshall (15) 120
Isha Dhanjal (13) 122
Sid Vaidya (12) 124
Amina Zohra Riaz (13) 125
Maya Legge (13) 126
Alice Wilkinson (11) 127
Keeley Spencer (13) 128
Bella Whitty (12) 129
Saira Ramzan (12) 130
Isabella Smith (12) 131
Poppy Felin (13) 132
Sameen Ahmed (12) 133
Sophie Meredith (13) 134
Christopher Sondai (12) 135
Iqra Khan 136
Ottilie Carter (12) 137
Gabriel Wilkinson (14) 138
Chloe Enock (11) 139
Penelope Wilkinson (12) 140
Kirsten Kabanga Mpemba Nsendu 141
Hannah Armour (17) 142
Davina Ema Udoh (11) 143

The Purcell School, Bushey

Elsa Rapisarda (15) 144
Ella Richardson (14) 145

THE POEMS

MARS

Oh Mars, the faraway, sombre land
Covered in red sand
You seem to glow
You're the place no one can go
The place many leagues away from us
The thing no one can touch

Oh Mars, the great beast of war
Moved by an unseen hand
I watch you rise and fall
I feel your fiery breath on me
You are hot, dry and unforgiving
You are a maker of death

Oh Mars, the red sombre land
You are so grand
You seem to command
And understand
Everything that goes on
Down in our land.

Hilton D

MASKED

You see my skin, the flesh I try to hide
My skin as cold as ice, my skin as dark as night
And you flinch, aghast at what you see
I'm dangerous, unwanted in your country
Because I'm new, I'm stealing all your jobs
I'm taking what's not mine and I'm getting what I want
And in that mind of yours, you spin this epic tale
We can stop them coming, stop this major scale
You think I'm bad, infectious and need to be contained
But you only see my surface, the reputation I've obtained
But really I'm just begging and trying to ask for help
As I'm scared for my family, I'm scared for myself
Yet I'm discriminated against as I'm simply not the same
As you believe you're superior, better than us in every way
You have these stories conjured up in your mind
About all of those people you are taught to despise
Little do you know, you taint their prestige
How they are seen by all of society
Then they are turned back around, back on their way
Back to poverty and despair, forced astray
You see those poor children up on the screen
Crying and drinking water which isn't clean
But you don't really think, you don't really care
As it doesn't affect you, you've got more than your fair share
Years and years onwards, we are still stuck in the past

Still making stereotypes, still judging people so fast
You make people feel less than because of their race
When they cannot help the colour of their face
So I'm telling you now to try to fix your mistake
Before you're just a number of people who were too late.

Lauren Lisk (13)

Dame Alice Owen's School, Potters Bar

THE SHALLOW MIND

A torrent of hurtful comments drown her,
They think it's a joke and just can't infer,
That what they are saying is nasty and mean,
She hides her tears, she doesn't want them to see,
That what they are saying is tearing her apart,
Like fragments of glass it's shattering her heart.
She tries to lose weight, she really does,
But instead of encouraging they laugh and they cuss.
Little do they know she cries herself to sleep,
Now she feels stupid, a loser, a creep.
They are judgemental - can't see past her facade,
She's beautiful inside but everyone is flawed.
No one really knows her but no one really cares,
They just condemn her for her looks and compare them to theirs.
She's cocooned inside blocking all the hate,
Just stop judging now - before it's too late.
You can stop her sorrow and eventually halt her cries,
Before all hope left inside her finally dies.

Simran Misir (12)
Dame Alice Owen's School, Potters Bar

AN ODE TO ADVENTURE

This is to the feeling of flying through the air,
To carefree laughter and tangled up hair,
This is to the pain of badly scraped knees,
And the giddy freedom, of doing as you please.

This is to the agony of watching someone fall,
To clenching your jaw, and giving it your all,
This is to the love you feel, holding someone tight,
Gazing at the stars, dancing through the night.

This is to the fury, burning through your veins,
To good and bad, love and loss, happiness and pain,
This is to the beauty of the winter snow,
And the quiet peace, of finally letting go.

This is to bravery, this is to fun,
This is to shouting and marching as one,
This is to life, blazing and bright,
This is to adventure, and I hope you do it right.

Natalie Kuper (14)
Dame Alice Owen's School, Potters Bar

ADVENTURE

I see scarecrows, leaves
I can hear the wind howling, the leaves crunching
I can smell pine, rain and the fruit growing on the trees
As I reach out I can feel crunchy leaves floating in the air
I can feel the chilly air, the wet, damp ground beneath my feet.

I start playing hide-and-seek
Then I find a magical fairy dancing, singing around
Singing at the top of her lungs,
I freeze on the spot.

I just stood there, thinking, *what a magical fairy,*
Am I dreaming as I gaze at this fairy?
I feel like I have just had an amazing dream.

G C (15)
Priory Hospital School High Wycombe, High Wycombe

ADVENTURE

Blowing into the crisp air, we start to drift;
We hover for a second in the breeze,
Our hair as thin and soft as a beautiful piece of snow.
We remind ourselves of warm, crisp, soft air,
We walk bare-footed into a breeze of soft, thin beach
With the brightest sand you've ever seen.
We enter a paradise island with a sun as hot and as big as a desert.
We've had a long day; we gaze into the midnight sky in the soft, breezy beach, ready for the next day.
The island looks just like this at night and at daytime.

S H (16)
Priory Hospital School High Wycombe, High Wycombe

ADVENTURE

It's the year 2118;
I hear the buzzing from the drone, finally, it has arrived.
Now beans get delivered from Mars
And they don't come in cans anymore.
The sauce is a powder
And the beans are dried up haricot beans.
We have machines that hydrate them,
This is the same with all foods.
They are ready to eat now.
They do not taste the same anymore,
They have different flavours now;
Fish, chicken, sausage and beef.
Beef's my favourite.
What is the world coming to?

Blake J (15)
Priory Hospital School High Wycombe, High Wycombe

WE MUST DO BETTER

There are things going on in the world and people turn a blind eye,
Some caused by women, some caused by guys.
Murders or kidnappings, they all have something in common,
When something new pops up the previous ones become forgotten.
Unfortunately, all of these usually end in bloodshed,
And usually, someone lying on a hospital bed.
Why are people so cruel? We must do better,
Let us start a new routine that shall become a trendsetter.
But we all know that it's not going to last,
And before you know it, it's blown away into the past.
Then someone else starts again with the havoc and destruction,
And *poof!* there's already been another abduction.
It'll follow up with theft and it'll follow up with fights,
And people who can't stick their life would be jumping off of heights.
So what worthy life have we all built to live,
If pain and anguish are all we know to give?

Kemi Soyele (12)
Putteridge High School, Luton

THE FLUFFY RABBIT

One day, a little rabbit went out to play,
He called his friends through his fence,
And said, "Come play with me today!"
Together him and his friends
Sat on their hay,
Looking through the lens,
While eating Taco Bells.
They went on a woodland adventure,
And met a funny little creature.
It was a ladybug with spots as its feature,
Together they went to the city,
It was very busy,
People going to their jobs,
And then they found their caterpillar friend, Bob,
They all went to the Target shop,
To buy a yummy lollipop,
Fluffy Rabbit, Bob and his friend all walked home,
On the way, they went to Starbucks to get a coffee topped in foam.
They all went home on their separate ways,
To go to bed and do it all over again.

Ami Catherine Giles (12)
Putteridge High School, Luton

THE FUTURE

The future is the question which guides our existence.
An action to take, a plan to make,
Is a road to build full of dreams,
Drawn with the colours of life.

The future can have ups and downs,
Like roads around the countrysides.
It can be slow and it can be fast,
Easy or hard, sprinkled with the challenges of living.

The future is the way in which you see,
Your picture in time,
Is the light which gives you hope,
To carry on with your life.

Your steps all one by one,
Are added on to grow your heart,
The ways in which you live your life,
Are always an important part.

The future is like the blue sky,
Endless and full of life.
With clouds or sunshine,
But it can always make you smile.

Alessia Clapa (13)
Putteridge High School, Luton

THE QUEEN OF EGYPT

Many thousands of years ago in Ancient Egypt
A messenger was shipped
To see the queen at midnight
The iris of daylight
Cleopatra was her name
She is dead now (a shame)
But she was rumoured to be
A goddess you see.

Cleopatra bathed in milk
And nearly always wore dresses of the finest gold silk
As she swept through her mighty palace
She drank ice tea from a crystal chalice.

She teamed up with Julius and Mark
Caesar and Antony (missed out that part)
She was born after the pyramids and rocks
But definitely left her mark on the history books
Cleopatra was as mighty as the sphinx
But not as tough as most people think
Her death was brought to her by a snake
And the poison the asp dared to make.

Saphia Murray (11)
Putteridge High School, Luton

THE WONDER EYES

I can hear my heart beating in my chest.
I can hear the thoughts of my mind.
I can hear the drumming in my brain.
I can see the wonder in people's eyes.
I can see all of their fake smiles.
I can see them laughing.
I can feel the salty tears roll down my cheek.
I can feel my eyes scrunch up.
I can feel my black eyelashes clinging together.
I'm different.
However, people don't know that yet.
Unless they look at my face.
They all have that look of horror.
They all have that look of a forced smile.
They all run.
They all make noises and stare.
I know what I look like.
They know what I look like.
I wish they knew what I was like
But not just on the outside
But on the inside too.

Gracie Eve Coomber (11)
Putteridge High School, Luton

ADVENTURES ARE GREAT

Adventures are great,
Adventures are fun,
The thrills you get are far from none
Adventures get you up on your feet,
And you never know who you might meet.
You face challenges that make your heart race,
You see other things face to face.
You experience the best and worst of weather,
And there's no need to go alone,
Go as a group, together.
If going outdoors isn't your thing,
Well, that's just fine,
Find an adventure that's more worth your time,
It doesn't need to be big, no, not at all,
It could be something considered quite small.
Maybe like learning another language, yes that's right,
That is an adventure with the ups and the downs,
It may even keep you up all night.

Isabelle Johansson-Ward (11)
Putteridge High School, Luton

THE SOLAR SYSTEM AND HUMAN NATURE

The world is blue
And the sun is true,
From all the radiation, it will kill you.
The moon is a rock,
As a wormhole could suck.
The moon is light
As we're gonna make it dynamite.
The planets are big and small,
But humans are nowhere near tall
Humans can do silly things like a clown
But then again people just frown.
It's scary movies that make us do it
Because we give up and fall into the pit.
Life has open opportunities for us
Make sure we can spot those forgeries.
If it lets you down
Do shout as loud as a town
Because it will make you think of being an animal
But you think you know it all.
So feel proud, you are the hero,
Just work hard and don't give up.

Ayaan Uddin (14)
Putteridge High School, Luton

ADVENTURE ENJOY

A dventures can be exciting
D ays of fun and joy
V enturing through the world
E verybody can venture
N ever a dull place to go
T o the moon and back
U nusual places to explore
R unning around, having fun
E njoying ourselves.

There are so many places to enjoy
New places to explore
Mountains, rivers, jungles
All the places to explore in the world
Too many things to enjoy
Big or little, all are very enjoyable.

E njoyable times for all
N obody would want to miss an adventure
J oyous feelings enter your body
O nly adventures are this exciting
Y ou can be adventurous.

Sophie Browne (14)
Putteridge High School, Luton

THE FIELDS

The fields of poppies blowing in the wind
Hiding the bodies of our enemies, them forever sinned
We won wars but at what cost?
We wish we could bring back our loved ones, forever lost
New life hiding the scars of the past
But they will not be forgotten outcasts.

All the wars fought
Either won or lost
Life sucked away like a big drought
Sorrow spreading like icy frost
The fields of poppies blowing in the wind
Hiding the bodies of our enemies, them, forever sinned.

The clatter of guns filled the air
Men and women fighting like bears
Blood splattered and tired
The fields of poppies blowing in the wind
Hiding the bodies of our enemies, them, forever sinned.

Ben O'Hara (12)
Putteridge High School, Luton

ON THE WAY TO WONDERLAND!

It's started with a trip and a slip,
It was all too quick!
Down the rabbit hole it is!
There wasn't a mole.
I didn't know where I'd go.

"Mr Rabbit, Mr Rabbit, wait, wait, please!"
But I was too late, he already did leave.
Everything so large, except food
And to be honest, I was in the mood!

One bite is all I had
Then I got rather sad,
A giant I was, larger than doors,
I didn't know the laws.

I grabbed the key,
Ready to leave,
But how will I shrink back down?
I looked around,
Oh someone, save me now!
I drank the liquid, shrunk back down,
Wonderland, here I come now!

Madison-May Lena Orchard (11)
Putteridge High School, Luton

FEELINGS

Sad, angry, stressed,
Helpless, annoyed, frustrated.

When I found out the news I was upset,
I was angry,
It came to speaking to the person,
I was frustrated,
The day came where there was more information,
I was stressed,
It came closer to the time, four days before,
I felt helpless.

Sad, angry, stressed,
Helpless, annoyed, frustrated.

I keep thinking of all the good times,
Laughter, fun,
Exhaustion, silliness,
Pillow fights, baking.

Sad, angry, stressed,
Helpless, annoyed, frustrated.

All of these words
Mean one thing to me...

Cancer!
But my nan's a fighter!

Ellie May Worboys (12)
Putteridge High School, Luton

INTO ANOTHER WORLD

Running into the next generation
Where there are no trees, no greenery
Just houses and roads.
Light glowing at night from the ground.
Colourful buildings, it makes me feel dizzy.

This world has greenery everywhere
People have lives
OAP people alive
Medicines to fight disease
Modern schools
Gyms to be fit
Healthy choices.

This world has fun but not fun activities
Fast food where people eat
No gyms to keep lean
Nowhere to have fresh air
Gigantic buildings, taller than the sky
Obese people everywhere.

What is this world coming to?
I'm ashamed and scared
Fresh air makes a healthy life.

Eryn Phillips-Westcott (13)
Putteridge High School, Luton

THE FUTURE

The future, the future, people flying,
Flying cars, everyone is healthy,
No one will suffer.
Life will be simple,
No one will stress again.
Robots will deliver our shopping,
Any time,
Any day.
The future, the future, no one
Will fear again.

Robot police will patrol and care for us,
No one would be normal and be upset.
Happiness will be the only emotion existing.
Robot pets,
Self-driving cars with limited battery,
Teleportation and people flying everywhere,
Free money for everyone,
No one will be poor,
Everyone is kind, and no one is mean to others,
Everyone is kind and helpful.

Harvey Daniels (12)
Putteridge High School, Luton

MY PERFECT WORLD

In my perfect world, I can go where I like.
A walk up a mountain is certainly no hike.
But when I'm not in my world, nothing is right,
When I'm not in my world, every mountain's a fight.
When I close my eyes I'm in my perfect world,
Nothing is straight because everything is twirled.
In my world everything is free,
Anything and everything I can see.
Every day of every year,
The sun is always shining.
Every day of every year,
The sun can almost be blinding.
Nothing is left in my perfect world,
Because everything is right.
Nothing is dark in my perfect world
Because everything is bright.

Libby Bennett (11)
Putteridge High School, Luton

LOST IN THE JUNGLE

Haiku Poetry

Crashing through the vines,
I have done this seven times,
Lost in the jungle.

Trying to get out,
Tigers, poison and the heat,
Lost in the jungle.

Which way can I turn?
My skin feels like it may burn,
Lost in the jungle.

No people in sight,
Cheetahs giving me a fright,
Lost in the jungle.

Trees are circling me,
All around me, can't escape,
Lost in the jungle.

Help me, I am lost,
Bats are flying around me,
Lost in the jungle.

Anxious and worried,
Running through this dreadful place,
Lost in the jungle.

Rebecca Gibson (11)
Putteridge High School, Luton

PAST AND THE FUTURE...

Our past we can't control,
It's over and done.
No way to recover time,
Those days are gone.

No use of moaning over the past,
Regretting all those days,
No need to get untangled
In memory's purple haze.

The future is uncertain,
No way for us to see,
The things holding for you
Or for me!

Now, is what's obtainable,
Just moments here to share.
The future comes so quick,
Unseen but waiting there.

Seize the present moments,
Grab all that we can contain!
Our futures are elusive,
Our past we cannot chain!

Aryan Reid (12)
Putteridge High School, Luton

YOU'RE A JOY

Your eyes are like rhinestones,
Your hair like silk,
You look like life itself,
What a joy it must be.

My eyes are like pearls,
My hair like velvet,
I look like life itself
Or so I hear from you.

You compliment your peers,
You strive for success,
Your popularity matters,
Your friends help with all.

I compliment my peers,
I strive for success,
My popularity doesn't matter,
I'm cool with where I am.

You love everyone,
That includes me,
I thank you for that,
You're a real dear to me.

Isabella Cowell (12)
Putteridge High School, Luton

THE OCEAN

I think about the future,
And what will happen to the sea,
The pollution, the plastic,
It is tragic to me.

Help us spread awareness, turn the tide on plastic,
To cleanse our ocean, that would be fantastic,
It's destroying our beaches and our fish too,
The home that they live in needs to be blue,
All it needs is our time and devotion,
To remove the terrible mess from our beautiful ocean,
Plastic isn't dissolvable,
But it is recyclable so do your bit and don't litter it,
Save our oceans today.

Jojo Moloney (11)
Putteridge High School, Luton

INNER FEELINGS

L oving someone means leaving space for them in your life.
O nly one you really love,
V ery important to have a husband or wife.
E veryone deserves to be asked to the dance.

S adness is not funny.
A ll people should be happy.
D on't be sad or mad, be glad.

F unny people all around you,
U nder the weather is somewhere not many people should be.
N o one should be sad.
N o one should be mad.
Y ou can cheer up anyone, just try.

Adel Leona Toth (12)
Putteridge High School, Luton

FRIENDSHIP

The feeling of friendship from the start
Is that feeling in your heart
They make you happy when you're sad
A friend is there through good and bad

Are we friends or are we not?
You told me once but I forgot
Of all the friends I've ever met
You're the one I won't forget

And if I die before you
I'll go to Heaven and wait for you
I hope that you can see
You're a total joy to me.

There isn't a thing I wouldn't do
To have a friend just like you.

Shreeya Radia (12)
Putteridge High School, Luton

THE FUTURE

The future, the future
There may be a lot.
The future, the future
Give it all you've got.
The future, the future
It's all about life.
The future, the future
Forget about your wife.
The future, the future
Do what you've got to do.
The future, the future
Go and be you.
The future, the future
It may be really tough.
The future, the future
Forget that it's rough.
The future, the future
What you are about.
The future, the future
Go on and get out.

Jamie Thomas Croot (13)
Putteridge High School, Luton

WHEN IT GETS HERE

When it gets here,
What will it be?
Oh, I wonder,
Is the future near?

Alien invasion,
Robotic war,
Disease...
What horrors shall we face?

How big will phones be?
When will hover cars come?
Will Trump have finished his wall?
Has ISIS gone?

Will cyborgs walk the Earth?
Can everyone breathe?
Will Pluto be colonised?
Oh, what will the future hold?

What medical breakthroughs?
What technical advances?
Will it be great when it gets here?

Alex Gibson (13)
Putteridge High School, Luton

THE FORTNITE COMPETITION

Today is Fortnite day
We're going away on a coach
With Fortnite clothes
Getting ready for a battle royale
Up against a scout
Hope they aren't hard
Otherwise, I'll try hard
Shooting the cube
To kill some noobs
But the cube shot me
So all the noobs can see
I lost the game
What a shame
I'll be back
With no lack of concentration
You better be ready
And get steady
I'll be back for the scout
And you'll see I'll get the victory royale!

Daniel Adewale Akinyemi (11)
Putteridge High School, Luton

DEATH, DESTRUCTION

D astardly war
E pic ways to go out
A wesome, torturous tendencies
T orture that brings you to the edge of suicide
H ail the god that ends it all, you are done

D ie and go away
E xcruciating pain
S uicide takes you away
T ell no one
R est in peace
U ndeniable pain
C ontinued torture
T errible tonsillitis gives you pain
I ncredible ink poisoning
O bvious pain
N o escape.

Steven James Wilson (14)
Putteridge High School, Luton

HATE

Hate will burn and crush all happiness
And demolish all your love.
It will smash all of your joy
And kill the good inside you.
It incinerates your memories of all the good times
With friends and family
And you get it by someone being mean to you
Or stress from all your worries
And the only way to get rid of it is to forget about it
And be happy.
But hate will try and stop you
And make you run and hide
But if you forget about it all
It will let you be happy.

Jake Breheny (11)
Putteridge High School, Luton

WINTER

The ground glistens,
The silence listens,
Soft cotton-like drops fall,
Snow-capped trees stand tall.

Crisp glass-like ice trickles down as sharp canes,
Intricate crystallisation forms along windowpanes,
The soft, crisp flakes settle like angel feathers,
I love the bright, heavenly weather.

Warm hot chocolate with whipped cream,
A sweet winter dream,
A soft, warm glow grows around me,
The ground glistens,
The silence listens,
Winter.

April Brown (13)
Putteridge High School, Luton

THERE WAS A GIRL

There was a girl,
Who had lots of friends,
But then they all switched up,
She was left alone in the end.

She cried for hours,
Watching messages roll through,
'You should kill yourself, everyone hates you'.
She kept quiet for days, days upon months.

Her mum didn't know why she was acting up,
Tried to talk to her kid,
But her kid felt like giving up,
Mum started crying,
She didn't understand why her child felt like dying.

Serena Mepani (14)
Putteridge High School, Luton

SOON AFTER

As meetings take place with people who are ready,
To help many others who can't share a penny.
As time goes on, there are many donations.
And those without will cheer in jubilation.

As assemblies occur and some children are bored,
Little do they know there is so much more,
As when they grow up, they will see,
That what they saw was important indeed!

And it would be nice for people to be keen
On the changes which occur soon after they're seen.

Adam Tirletti (12)
Putteridge High School, Luton

ADVENTURE

This adventure is part of history
And it all started with a mystery.
A map towards an adventure
And not all stories end with treasure.

Happiness and laughter on the way there,
Stepping on the green grass, smelling the fresh air.
On a boat towards an island,
Long grass and big trees on the land.

Games and challenges, so unfair,
Now we have to split up in pairs.
Fighting each other until the end,
Who will last and who will end?

Chloe Angel Remorin (12)
Putteridge High School, Luton

MY NAN!

My nan is so old,
But she has a happy soul,
And I don't know how old she is today.

She helps me for school,
Even though it is a bore
And she irons my shirts too.

My nan is amazing,
She can be a bit basic,
Even though she's old today.

My nan is so old,
But she has a happy soul,
And I don't know how old she was the other day.

She can do anything.
My nan!
My nan!

Leo Howard Geoffrey Scott (11)
Putteridge High School, Luton

AN ODE TO A TREE

Tree, tree, standing so tall,
Proving breathtaking views for us all,
Pear, oak, apple and birch,
So many to choose, my eyes hurt.

Sitting under the leafy canopy,
I couldn't think of a better fantasy,
At first, a blush of brown and green,
Once you get closer there's more to be seen.

Climbing up the trustworthy branch,
Once you get to the top there'll be a wonderful glance.

Katie Behrens (12)
Putteridge High School, Luton

THE LIGHTS BEGAN TO FLICKER

The lights began to flicker
So I ran quicker
As pitch-black surrounded me
The eyes were following me.

As light in the distance began to grow
But where would this path even go?
Deeper into the woods
Where no creature should.

Out from the cave of nightmares
Little did I know the place beyond, full of scares
Monsters, creatures and sorrow...
But that is a story for tomorrow.

Kate Starkey (12)
Putteridge High School, Luton

FEELINGS

Strolling through the woods
Surveying my surroundings
Animals hopping joyfully in the grass
Birds chirping and singing a merry song
Trees dancing in the breeze
The beauty makes me sneeze.

As I stroll deeper and deeper
I get the feeling I'm being watched by a creeper
Then I come across a shed
Which is made of lead
The darkness that it is surrounded by
Makes me want to cry.

James David Armour (14)
Putteridge High School, Luton

INNER FEELINGS

Happiness towers over the darkness and doubt.
Sadness is constantly dragging toward death.
Anxiety controls my swift movement and grumpiness fills my heart.
The never-ending worries never escape.
These are inner feelings
Then I discover it's a reality.
Yet another day when emotions suddenly take control.
Confidence slowly rises to the top.
Anger rapidly changes the perspective of life.

Scarlet Samantha Louise O'Dell (12)
Putteridge High School, Luton

I WONDER

Every day I wonder,
What the future will be like?
If there will be any cars or bikes,
Or if there will be technology that's new,
Will the sky always be blue,
With snow, white clouds,
That are not so loud?

Every day I wonder,
If there will be any toys,
For the young girls and boys,
Or will there be any video games?
All we know is that nothing will be the same.

Riyana Mepani (11)
Putteridge High School, Luton

A DAY OUT

Today is our holiday
The day we go away
The time for family time
And the time where the beach is mine
The sun, the atmosphere
The sea is so clear
Oh, how wonderful it is to be here.

Leaving the beach was so sad
I would love to go back there so bad
Maybe next week, don't worry
But all I thought was...
We don't have enough money.

Bethel Obuseh (12)
Putteridge High School, Luton

DINNER TONIGHT

Chicken and chips,
Chicken and chips,
Tomato ketchup all over my lips.
Chew, chew,
Yum, yum,
Into my tum.

Banana split,
Banana split,
When I have it,
I lose it.
Chew, chew,
Yum, yum,
Into my tum.

Dinner tonight,
Dinner tonight,
It should be great.
Dinner tonight,
I can't wait!
It should be great.

Luke Joshua Whiting (12)
Putteridge High School, Luton

THE GIRL

As I look around the room,
My mind keeps hearing these loud booms,
I wish I knew what she felt,
What if she reveals

The secrets she's been hiding?
So I feel like I'm dying,
If I find out the truth
But I'll feel so rough.

Maybe I'll cry,
Or she could say bye.
If she runs
I will always come.

Joe Field (12)
Putteridge High School, Luton

BASKETBALL

I like sports
Sports are the best
My favourite sport is basketball
And I'm not going to change.

My favourite basketball player
Is Michael Jordan
Because I think he's the best.

Michael Jordan is a really good player
He got a lot of scores in a match
No one else can stop him
Because he's the best.

Peter Schneider (12)
Putteridge High School, Luton

JASPER

My dog's name is Jasper,
He is the master,
He loves to play
During the day.

We take him to the vets,
He loves playing with pets,
When we settle down for the night,
He wakes up in the morning light.

I love my dog,
He loves me,
We will be together
Until we're twenty.

Daisy Brown (11)
Putteridge High School, Luton

ADVENTURE

I wake up from out of my bed,
Wondering what adventures will be ahead,
I dream of touching the clouds and the sky,
But then I realise I can't fly,
I think about going to the beach today
And then I remember it's too far away,
I hope to go somewhere else one day,
However, that might not be the way.

Mia Dehnert (12)
Putteridge High School, Luton

THE JUNGLE

Monkeys swinging from trees,
Rain falling on leaves.

Birds flying high,
Chicks try to fly.

Trees growing tall,
Hearing tigers call.

Exploring far and near,
While driving behind a rear.

Sneaky snakes slithering on the ground,
And hissing very loud.

Nasra Daoud (12)
Putteridge High School, Luton

FEELINGS

Don't bully,
Bullying is bad,
It makes people sad,
The depression is mad.
Tell teachers
Or your mum and dad.

If it affects you a lot,
Give all the strength you've got,
If you're not feeling right
You don't need to fight,
Just stay strong.

Tegan Sarah Jo Ridey (13)
Putteridge High School, Luton

I DIDN'T WANT TO WRITE THIS POEM

Roses are red
Violets are blue
I didn't want to write this poem
But I was made to.

Roses are red
Violets are blue
Twenty lines of this
Would be cuckoo.

Roses are red
Violets are blue
I'm done with this poem
And you should be too.

Liam Stoll (13)
Putteridge High School, Luton

SCHOOL

School is fun,
School is cool,
School is for everyone,
Welcome for all.

The teachers are funny,
Cool and talented,
They teach us a lot,
We should be thankful.

Putteridge is the best school,
Welcome for all,
Large, tall,
Even the small.

Ela Yilmazgul (11)
Putteridge High School, Luton

MY CATS

My cats are crazy
One's called Jasmine,
The other one, Marley.
Jasmine scratches the carpet,
Then runs and gallops around like a horse,
She's gone crazy.
Marley on the other hand,
Likes to lick your shoes.
When she sees food
She will meow at you!

Libbie Conquest (11)
Putteridge High School, Luton

THE FUTURE

There might be hoverboards,
There might be no planes,
But trust me, they are going to put us to shame.
The world may end or blow up
So you may as well suck it up.
There may be spy gadgets and flying bikes
But don't be scared,
It will not bite.

Oliver Johnson (13)
Putteridge High School, Luton

SCHOOL SUCKS

School is bad,
It drives me mad,
Teachers are phonies,
They dream about ponies.
Uniform sucks, you have to tuck it in,
Homework sucks because you have to do it at home.
We go to school for six hours a day...
What's your problem bro?

Joshua Bush (11)
Putteridge High School, Luton

THE POWER OF LOVE

Love is a strange feeling
That no one understands,
It takes control of you
Whenever it wants.

I know it's hard
But it's something you have to overcome,
You can't ignore it
Because it always comes back.

Asfia Khan (14)
Putteridge High School, Luton

A LOOK INTO THE FUTURE

The future seems to be getting brighter every day
With everything going on at the moment
Time will definitely fly by
Whilst the world is spinning
For as long as it lives
Which could maybe last forever
But who knows?

Lewis Pedder (13)
Putteridge High School, Luton

SCHOOL

S chool is where you learn.
C an we finish the test now?
H istory is boring, why do we have to learn it?
O ne pen and pencil.
O ranges for snacks.
L eaving school at three.

Harvey Ben Taylor (11)
Putteridge High School, Luton

THE MONSTERS

You've heard about the monsters
That hide under our beds,
Or the ones that haunt the adults,
The ones inside their heads.

The ones that plague your dreams at night,
The ones you find in books,
The ones that give up on you,
The ones that criticize your looks.

The ones that change your loved ones,
Into something you despise,
The ones that disrupt your thoughts,
The ones that tell you lies.

The ones that can kill you,
With a blade or with a knife,
The ones that can use poison,
To make you give up on life.

No monster can disappear,
They're always lurking in the dark,
But they can be pushed away,
To the very edge of our hearts.

The monster that has found me though,
Isn't found in a book,

Doesn't appear in my nightmares,
Isn't something you overlook.

My monster doesn't play games,
Or keep me company in my mind,
It doesn't let me leave its sight
And doesn't leave me behind.

My monster is different,
One that nobody can escape,
It's the one I see in the mirror,
The one that took my place.

Sophia Mikou (13)

Queenswood School, Brookmans Park

FANTASY DREAM

Night falls, the moon rises, my eyes close,
An ideal world emerges,
So pretty, slim I am,
So cheerful, confident I am,
So enthusiastic, talented I am,
Like Taylor Swift, my idol.

Lights on, the curtain opens, microphones on,
The concert begins,
Singing with beautiful voice and melody,
To express the true emotion from the body.
Dancing with steady steps and rhythm,
To spread out the passion to the audience,
Taylor Swift and I, showing the talent,
Which we have the pleasure to be given,
Taylor Swift and I, showing the effort,
With our desire to succeed
And give back to fans for their love and support.

A new day begins, the sun rises, my eyes open,
This ideal world disappeared,
But my faith still stays,
Get the power from Taylor Swift,
To be the unique one, to be the best.

Taylor Tao (17)
Queenswood School, Brookmans Park

THE OCEAN

The ocean, plain and innocent,
But we act as if it is the sea maleficent!
Throwing plastic, treating it like dirt,
If it was your property, you'd probably shout and blurt!

Is this how you want our oceans to be?
Sea creatures dying whilst you're sipping on tea.
Whilst us humans enjoy our life,
Sea creatures are trying to let go of their worry and strife!

Do you really want our oceans to be brown?
Making all the lovely tourists frown!
Do you want polluted water to cause harmless animals death?
Imagine what it would be like witnessing their last breath?

Recycle your plastic,
This isn't a joke, it's drastic!
Help the sea life, they don't deserve to be extinct.
Please help so things like tsunamis are easier to predict.

Lisa Okrah (11)
Queenswood School, Brookmans Park

WHY?

Why is this me?
The monster that lies within,
Shouting and screaming in my head,
Words I once thought were untrue,
Now, I think they define me.

Why do people try to talk to me about it?
They try to destroy the monster,
That eats away at me,
Everything I do to numb the pain within,
Makes the monster shout louder.

Why do I try?
What has my life become,
That I have turned to drugs,
To stop the screaming,
Inside my head?

Why do I live?
Why do I bother?
Why should I care?
Why does no one care?
Why can't I just die?

Sophia Evans (12)
Queenswood School, Brookmans Park

WHAT I SAW

I saw you with her.
Why were you not with me?
I felt like you were the logger and I was the tree.
I yelled at you,
You tried to explain,
But nothing you said could have eased the pain.
I never talked to you,
Until that day,
We talked about life and the delay.
We agreed to be friends,
But nothing more,
Nothing would stop me forgetting what I saw,
We have taken our own paths,
We keep in touch.
I have forgiven you but not that much.

Darcy Evangeline Cheesman (11)
Queenswood School, Brookmans Park

YOU MADE HER SO SURE

(Haiku poetry)

You made her so sure
The sun had come to join us
Down here on this Earth

Although you were lost
Just a star in the distance
She wouldn't lose hope

You shattered her heart
Thunder cracked and then the storm
Lightning struck her life

Oceans filled her eyes
A hurricane of sorrow
Drowning in her tears.

Amber Smith (13)
Queenswood School, Brookmans Park

BALLOON

The perfect blue of the sky,
I spot something right up high.

I squint and blink to grab a look,
Like a child reading a picture book.

And then I see it, golden brown,
Beautiful patterns twisting in and out.

A large basket flying over my head,
And a giant balloon stitched with thread.

Around the globe,
Not too quickly nor too slow.

This hot air balloon has been
Travelling to places I'll never see.

On a little adventure of its own
Loving every place it'll ever go.

A small hot air balloon up high,
A small balloon in the sky.

Evie Simons (12)
Royal Latin School, Buckingham

A LOOKING GLASS

A looking glass
An unknown woe
The silence
Waiting, just waiting for a foe.

And then a jolt,
A sudden creak,
There is no dancing
In the street.

The door opens,
A shadowy figure,
Something huge,
Something bigger.

Bigger than a giant,
Bigger than a tower,
The house is so quiet,
He thinks he's in power.

And then he walks in,
Waiting for someone to appear,
But no one does,
The coast is clear.

He slowly walks
Along the floor,

Like a tiger,
Prowling on the moor.

Then he is gone,
No trace, no mask,
But what's here no more...?
A looking glass.

Lara May Evans (11)
Royal Latin School, Buckingham

INNER FEELINGS

I'm as happy as can be,
I passed my GCSE,
I got a new cat,
I named him Pat,
I'm as happy as can be!

I'm as annoyed as can be,
The cat got my tongue,
And I got stung by a wasp
Who was having his tea,
I'm as annoyed as can be!

I'm as glad as can be,
I just caught my bus,
Cos I was in a fuss,
I'm as glad as can be!

Kerensa Telford-Johns (11)
Royal Latin School, Buckingham

BEFORE IT'S TOO LATE

We are fettered to war,
Farewell peace,
Fighting for evermore,
No safety catch to release.

Our world is dying,
No glimpse of hope,
No more government lying,
A tightened noose made of rope.

The disease is rife,
Conflict or death, the only option,
Fighting for a shred of life,
Conflict or death, the only option.

Finn McGarr (11)
Royal Latin School, Buckingham

IN THE FOREST

I'm sitting on the forest floor,
Where no foot has been before,
You can see a pitch-black cave,
Where there lives a slave.

The cave ruled by the king,
Who has a boy called Bing,
He likes to dance and play,
During the day.

But he cannot do this,
As he is the slave in the cave.

Freyja Barker (12)
Royal Latin School, Buckingham

A FLOWER HAS BEEN BORN

Planting a seed, amongst the weeds,
Nurturing the flower, hour by hour,
Patting the earth, one of nature's many births,
Keeping it in the warm, away from any storm,
Petals soon bloom, creating life in a single room,
A rose without a thorn, a flower has been born.

Jaskiran Munde (11)
Royal Latin School, Buckingham

A RIDER'S DAY

Hark, the larks sing,
Where shall I ride today? I think.
Across the rocky slopes of the mountainside
Or in the grassy meadows, where my horse thrives?
I choose the place we both love so much,
On the forest trails, where wildlife runs free.

Chloe Elkins (11)
Royal Latin School, Buckingham

ESCAPE

Escape to see wonders you hear,
Escape to see and play by ear.

Escape and hear and be free,
Escape to see and find the key.

Walk among the sea waters,
And to also see the still waters.

Olivia Aggreh (12)
Royal Latin School, Buckingham

RAINFOREST

The air is heavy, thick and still,
So still I can feel a frog leap from across the makeshift path,
So heavy and thick I can hear my heart pumping,
And feel my thoughts running away.

As I hike, the warm rain falls on my face,
Drizzling down like a waterfall.
The colossal trees looking down at me screech,
From the life they contain.
Great orangutans sway past me,
As if they were challenging me to a race.
Large, lush leaves lapse,
Whilst wild weather wails.

As I walk on, I feel the soft, wet ground,
Cradling my feet.
The mist distorts my vision from seeing the waterfall,
Until I get closer and stare in awe at the water roaring down the cliff face.

Loud cracks of thunder boom and crash in the deep blue sky,
Sending the birds frantically fleeing their trees.
Vibrant neon frogs dart across the ground,
While beetles scurry around my feet.
I approach an ear-splitting river,
Which is begging me to cross it.

I voyage across it, spotting a leaping fish,
Splashing up cool water at me as it crashes to the water surface.
Bugs fly around me, preying on my sweat,
And tearing into my skin.
I jaunt up to an opening,
At which I see a vivid toucan soar down to feast on fallen fruit.

I advance to a nearby cliff and sit down,
My legs swinging carelessly over the edge.
I look across the vast sea of trees,
Spotting a man yell, "Timber!" at the top of his lungs,
Whilst a tree falls.
Birds scatter,
Monkeys wail,
And leopards dart,
From their destroyed dwellings.

Henry Macer (12)
Sibford Senior School, Sibford Ferris

I AM YOUR FEELINGS

Hello. Welcome to the world little one
I am your feelings,
I will always be there for you.
We can feel together.
We can be happy. We can be sad.
That's it right now.

We feel older.
Everything is smaller.
We could scream right now if we like
Come on, let's.

That new girl's nice.
Let's try and make her laugh.
That went very well.
We are getting better at this.

Everything is so loud and angry.
Mum is making us angry.
Scream at her, now!
Now run away, good, good,
Slam the door, perfect.
You are doing very well.

We feel older again.
We want to go.
We should leave right now.
We should run, run and be free.

It's cold, we miss Mum and Dad.
We want to go home.
That man just smiled at me.
He seems nice.
He's coming over, be cool.

We have been through loads together,
But he's here for you now.
I am so happy for you.
But I have to go now.
Goodbye, little one.

Maia Luxton (13)
Sibford Senior School, Sibford Ferris

MY SWEET MADNESS

I'm not content
Although I am content.

The scales and chains
I see before me

When I sleep
Only feelings speak to me

"Distress, distress,
This is not just in your head!"

This is what I hear
Being screamed at in my ear.

I'm only a puppet
For my mind to abuse.

Margot Connop (14)
Sibford Senior School, Sibford Ferris

HOLLOW

Awake, it's 2am, I am alone
Talking to the voices of the ghosts
And the sun rises,
A new day, but I ask,
Is this living?

I'll say I'm busy
But I'm desperately hiding under the sheets
Because I find the darkness comforting
But frightening,
Is this living?

I can't sleep, I'm awake with the skeletons,
Demons dancing around me,
I have a hollow chest, beating,
Is this living?

Anger runs through my veins, I am so lost,
Echoing the halls of my loose, limp wrists,
I am alone in desperate solitude.

This is living.

Kelly Lloyd (16)
Space Studio Banbury, Banbury

TSUNAMI

The giant within the Earth growled,
And then they told us it was coming
Waves of panic overwhelmed us,
For we knew what to expect.

We scrambled to the highest point,
Pushing and shoving like animals,
The stench of panic lingered in the air
Intoxicating us one by one,
Everyone filled with a sense of despair.

We left our lives behind,
No time, no time, no time.
And then they told us there was no risk,
And gave our lives back to us again.

When we got home the ocean had gone.
Backwards, backwards, backwards.
And then we knew what was to come; no mistake,
It was too late.

Too late to run; too late to hide, too late to climb our fears inside.
The tide came fast, high and vast.
Crashing, screaming, crushing everything in its way,
Taking all these lives away.

It dragged me; it battered me; it had no respect for life,
My lungs filled up with the dirty brown water.
Another score for mindless slaughter,
It chewed me up and spat me out.

"But I'm not one of its victims," I shout,
Not today, not again
Never will I listen when they say, "When..."
I'll listen to the giant instead,
And that way I will not be one of Palu's 800 dead.

My mother, my brother, my home...
All washed away
The death toll still rising, can't they hear the crying?
People lost, people found
Each one of them wearing a silent frown,
Rigid, bloated, frigid,
Darkness falling as they drowned.

But I'm neither lost nor found,
I have the right to wear my frown,
Although I have nowhere to go, no one to see,
Only other people like me,

We know we are the lucky ones,
The ones who remain free...
Free from the wave, free from the water,
Free from death, free from slaughter.

Help is arriving one week later,
Medicine, food and clean water,
But too late for those who weren't found
The death toll doubled; more rotting on the ground.

Eilidh Colla (12)
St Margaret's School, Bushey

I KNOW WHAT IT'S LIKE

I know what it's like for strangers to want you dead,
They would happily point a gun to your head,
And shoot with the label etched in their brain,
Without even knowing as much as your name.

I know what it's like for people to hate you,
They base it on your race, not what you do.
They don't care about your petty pleas,
Even if it had you begging at your knees.

I know what it's like to feel trapped,
It feels like the truth is fabric wrapped.
If I dare make mistakes in this solemn planet,
Then my chest will be covered in liquid scarlet.

I know what it's like to be afraid,
Maybe history will be replayed.
All it takes is good people to be silent,
To cause the whole world to be violent.

I know what it's like to be a Jew,
That's what my poem is telling you.
A rerun of history isn't beyond fate,
So stop the hate before it's too late.

Beanie Bond-Ryde (12)
St Margaret's School, Bushey

BLINDED

We have been blinded from the truth.
We follow like sheep behind a shepherd
We rely on the word of others and not our wits.
Even though the truth is plainly there.
We pretend it is not a situation we must attend to,
Or a way in which we must change.

To us, living in our world is beautiful and free of complication
Whilst others live in fear and trepidation,
In anticipation of the enemy to make their next move
And a realisation that their futures could disappear in seconds.
Whilst others have nothing: no home, food or families
Whilst the ruthless hunt the innocent creatures
And cut down the trees, and destroy habitats

Isn't there a point that we will stop?
We have stolen the treasure and vibrancy of the reefs
We have stolen the diamonds from the night sky's cloak
We have stolen lives of this very Earth for the sakes of our own.
But although we think our intentions are blameless, innocent
How are we so naive that we brush off the realities of what we are truly doing?

Slowly the Earth has descended into more chaos, pain, destruction, jealousy and anger,

We are ruining the lives of our children and our children's children.
We are taught not to do these deeds but do them regardless.
Surely this guilt we cannot abide,
This guilt that we secretly hide?
This guilt and this lie that we hide from even ourselves
We have been blinded from the truth.

Lauren Crush (12)
St Margaret's School, Bushey

OBAMA IS ALWAYS IN OUR HEARTS WHILE TRUMP IS TRYING TO TEAR US APART!

Trump, help us understand
Lend the world a helping hand,
Ruling America is no game
When you make a mistake, don't say Obama is to blame.

All Obama's orders, you cancelled with a pen
Don't you care about America's men?
Isn't it scary that a man so repellent,
Could be in charge of nuclear deterrence?

"I'll build a great wall between Mexico and they will pay!"
But it's the Congress that will pay, that's what you said, just yesterday,
Putin's an enemy, he's not a friend
You need to make some serious amends.

Obama care is the greatest thing, I swear
Trump doesn't care about our health
All he wants is more wealth.

You're a drain on America's future
You have no feelings, just like a computer.

Obama had no political drama,
He was sweeter than a llama.

At first, we thought you were just a bloke
Who didn't care and had no hope,
Why take our money and leave us broke?
You really are the world's biggest joke.

All the energy you put into Twitter
Why not try being less bitter?
Obama never lost hope,
Even when in his heart, he couldn't cope.

Instead of dividing, please bring us together
The world is a small place, that won't last forever.
Please, Trump, listen to our advice,
Or it could lead to our terrible demise!

Roma Mehta (12)
St Margaret's School, Bushey

SHOTS OF MY REALITY

I'm not real
I feel way too much
I'm so numb that I can't feel
I try to fix the broken
But personally, haven't healed
I hate hearing sad songs
But they're really not sad at all.

Simply shots of my reality
Posted up on my wall
Not simple
But simply complicated
Half of my worries I created
Now I have to come and face it
But do I want to...? No!
Lately, I've been feeling more blue than black
I don't have a clock on it
Honestly, I haven't been keeping track.

My room is still
But I'm spinning, I still can't face the facts
Can't pay the bill, still taking pills
I'm feeling under attack
My heart's beating
My calm's leaving
Taking a deep breath, the only rest I seem to get
Look up to the sky, feel like I'm staring into space

Trying to win the race of life
Whose envision
My ears, ringing
My shine's dimming
I'm covered by all the clouds.

Tell the thunder to keep quiet
But the touching is too loud
I feel it rumbling the ground
My feet and my whole world begin to shake
Truth be told, I don't know how much trembling I can take
I can try
Man, I bet you, I could cry a river and a lake
I lift my hand to slap me in the face
Because I hate it when I cry
So I scream until I break.

Sherlene Olayinka (13)
St Margaret's School, Bushey

SLAVE GIRL

Two towers strong of stone and brick,
Overlooking a field of flowers thick
Red and orange, green and blue,
All the colours bright, much like the city it was beside.

In one tower, frail and small,
Singing like an angel, a magical song.
Lay against the hard stone floor
A young girl trapped for evermore.

From her small window, flew by
An exotic blue bird flying high.
"Will I ever escape and be free
And explore the world with joy and glee?"

She worked all day, slaved all night,
Only to return to her tower without right.
Cooking, fanning, dusting, cleaning
Has been.

Young girl trapped in the tower as a slave,
Mysterious master, guards the grave.
Hope of escape, being torn apart
Desperation for freedom growing in her heart.

Will she risk her life to flee?
She gave no care, she wanted to be free.

There was no life for her here
Only desperation she could no longer bear.

Thunder roared but the sun soon grew bright,
Slave girl made it through the night.
Birds sang merrily and she was lost in delight
Slave girl was finally free
And her name was Clementine Debrite.

Lybah Aleem Ahmad (12)
St Margaret's School, Bushey

A NO HOPE BATTLE

The day we all dreaded,
A rainy, grey day
Took no hesitation and dawned upon us.

The journey to the doctor's room,
We wished went slower,
And so the dreadful news fell upon us.

Day after day,
We trekked to the monstrosity of a hospital,
Wondering which day would be the last.

All beautiful and precious moments,
We cherished and adored,
And heartbreaking moments, we tried to block out

Many tried to save her,
Everyone tried anything they could,
Countless operations and sleepless nights,
Just to give a loving little child a chance.

As the weeks flew by,
So did our hope,
Tearing our baby out of our grasp.

Then came the day,
An agonising phone call,
Rushed us to that monstrosity,
Only to lose the little hope we had left and our darling...

Saying goodbye was the most heart-wrenching task,
And we want everybody to know what this extraordinary battle was like,
A no hope battle.

Varsha Mahendran (13)

St Margaret's School, Bushey

CRACKED CHINA

The sirens go off
I hear Mum calling my name
Out after curfew
The robots will come
Lasers trained on any movement
Bang go the weapons
Another one gone

This is the year 2145
In the past there was hope
But now?
There is death
Damaged, dangerous and dark
Elephants and bees
Only in our dreams

Living in what was China
When it was finer
Moving forward but
Regressing through time
Decay closing in
No time to be claustrophobic
Hide before the land turns explosive

The stench of the dead permeates the room
Before, it affected me but not anymore
I try to imagine something good

But everything is misunderstood
I look into the past
When things could last
And the world had meaning

The sirens go off
Is it safe?
I breathe again
Mum creeps out
Then gives a shout
Bang go the weapons
Another one gone.

Amarleen Brar (12)
St Margaret's School, Bushey

HOPE

In an ocean of emptiness
Searching for some light,
But the ones you had loved,
Have vanished without a sight.

Searching for help
But no one will come,
Trying to find love again
But everyone is done.

But that doesn't matter
Because you clung onto hope,
Which means that inside your heart
You will be able to cope

Your heart can shatter
Over and over again,
Although hope remains
You want it to end

Inside you,
You want to break,
You want to hate them
For leaving you this way

With none to love
And none to hate

None to argue
Or see your fate

None to trust
None to shame
None to embarrass
And see your fame.

But where is hope?
Is it even a thing?
Is it inside me?
Can it make me a king?

Hope will guide you
Till the end,
And then my friend,
I will see you again.

Emer Brownleader (12)
St Margaret's School, Bushey

YESTERDAY WAS A BLUR...

Yesterday was a blur and it drifted away in an unbeatable fog.
I remember the broken baby bird, lost in a patch of deep blue and green thorns as waves of cracked promises crashed against the soul.
However, a ray of daylight shone through the clouds of loss and pain.

Today, eyes have been misted by the longing of a nest full of delicate feathers as the night's sun beams down from the heavens, and its sharp knife kept my dreams away from me.
The spoon's gentle scoop teases me back to my crib of clouds and comfort.

Tonight, the wonder of a story completed will wash my fear away with the world I once knew.
The calming sky sighs back at me as the scent of vanilla and honey fills the air and blocks out all Earth's mistakes and settles for another chapter over.

The dream of tomorrow, one that will never come true.
The thought of gold meeting turquoise,
Facing the sea with a sunrise, as the kitten purrs to the tune of a well-known melody, hummed by the starry sky like a honey bee as it builds a barrier between the castle and the beast's pollution, with their cry of hate.

Alone but peaceful. Lost but free.
Lost in a sea of dreams.

Kate Maynard

St Thomas More Catholic School, Bedford

YESTERDAY

Yesterday
A raincloud followed me like a lost dog.
The deep, dark blue sea of sadness swept me away with the fearsome waves,
Tears raced each other down my face.
In a flash, toppled down like Jenga, not sure if I could get up again.

Today
I was an unshifting sloth, lounging in my deckchair.
The sun smiled down on me with its biggest grin.
My fingers flopped onto the tableside.
I glued my eyes shut.
Lazing away, enjoying the blazing summer's day.

Tonight
I'm a bird taking flight for the first time.
Butterflies hastily pacing up and down inside me.
My head spinning like bees that do not know where to go.
Spread my wings, took a small gulp,
At the very top of the roller-coaster ride,
Ready, steady, go.

Tomorrow
I will be as ready as I'll ever be.
My head already filling up with the chorusing loud applause.
I would be swimming in a pool of a million shining stars.

My feet, tingling, unable to keep still.
The smile that spreads across my face will be unable to wipe off.
I will come to the end of my roller-coaster ride.

Satasha Angelica Kumari (12)
St Thomas More Catholic School, Bedford

POEM

Yesterday
Boredom struck me.
I felt like I had nothing to do, as there was darkness all around me.
Different noises came into my head and my breathing went slower.
Nothing really could take this boredom away from me as it felt like it was stuck with me forever.

Today
Tiredness came into my head.
All I could think about was getting comfortable on the sofa.
I kept sighting a reflection of my tiredness, just like it was on a spoon.
All I could imagine was a soft and fluffy cloud drifting in the air but finally, it all came to an end.

Tonight
I have slight excitement in my thoughts.
It tastes slightly sweet as the thoughts keep running into my head.
A slight touch of enjoyment starts filling up my head as I keep wondering of the following day.

Tomorrow
The thoughts of last night keep drifting back into my head.
I feel more excitement and enjoyment as I refresh my memory.

The colour red starts popping into my sight as I close my eyes.
Tomorrow is the day that I have been thinking about these past few days.
And I wouldn't have it any other way.

Sandra Kulovic (12)
St Thomas More Catholic School, Bedford

YESTERDAY...

Yesterday
I felt shattered, tired, sleepy, like a sleeping sloth that's slightly sleepy from its long day.
I felt purple inside; a colour that represents what I feel.
Dancing, walking, playing, cheerleading, shouting, working.
After all of that, it is no surprise that I'm tired.

Today
Crazy and excited is what I'm feeling.
My emotions are like a blender spinning inside my brain.
I'm excited about... the best sleepover with my best friend!
My feelings are like the sun in the sky, high, high in the sky.

Tonight
Scared, as scary as two bears, like a dinosaur with wings, a dragon with fur or just a scary dog.
Imagine those things all crowded around you, well, that's how scared I feel for tonight.
I am teaching five million people to dance!
Although... I love teaching people to dance.

Tomorrow
Tomorrow I would love to be at a mansion in Spain in 40° heat and just to top it all I want to be opening birthday presents.
I would feel ecstatic if that really happened.

Autumn Clare Theakstone (12)
St Thomas More Catholic School, Bedford

YESTERDAY...

Yesterday
I felt pain, the shape of the pain was like a decagon.
It was bloody gory red, the pain was as sharp as bull horns.

Today
I feel depressed, I feel like this because I had no breakfast.
I have a headache like a sharp knife with gore on it.
If I had to describe my feeling with the weather it would be a lightning storm with a tornado.

Tonight
I am going to make a famous anime in Tokyo.
It feels like my favourite thing has come to life.
I like it because anime is the main existence of my life!
If I were comparing it to taste, it would taste like spaghetti and meatballs from Heaven.

Tomorrow
I would like to be sleeping and eating at the same time,
dreaming about all of my favourite animes.
It would feel like Heaven.
It would be a galaxy of purple,
It would be a majestic eagle,
and it would sound like angels singing harmony!

Temiloluwa Ajao
St Thomas More Catholic School, Bedford

UNTITLED

Yesterday
I felt excited.
As excited as the sun waiting for the perfect hour to rise and shine.
Booming with reds and ambers on the far horizon.

Today
I was lazy.
It was too hot to sleep.
Furious snoring came from next door,
Was it a monster? Who knows.
It was as angry as the kettle boiling up the once still water.

Tonight
I will fly to the moon.
Isolated in the middle of a thousand stars.
To get away from the busy life of society
Wondering if they know I am gone.

Tomorrow
It will be Christmas Day, full of fun and celebration.
I look outside, there is a frosty igloo
Which could be home to an angry yeti.
My ears filling up with sounds of laughter.
I can feel it inside of me, my adrenaline is pumping.
I call it joy.

Aimee Williams
St Thomas More Catholic School, Bedford

WHAT?!

Yesterday
I was annoyed.
I felt like a long rectangle that was frustrated it was not square.
It was like there was a fly, buzzing and bothering me.
The world felt yellow, all bright and annoying.

Today
I feel positive.
The fly has been swatted and now I can concentrate.
I feel the sunshine in me.
Like a clean, non-stick frying pan, I feel ready.

Tonight
I am going to eat Wookie chops and slow roasted Ewok.
I'm now a fluffy rainbow-pooping unicorn,
With the sweet taste of weird animals in my mouth.
A chicken, bear and hair hybrid.

Tomorrow
I'd like to subjugate an alien species and enslave them.
I am satisfied and green
Like a happy, victorious baby seal.

Elliot Tempest (11)
St Thomas More Catholic School, Bedford

YESTERDAY...

Yesterday
I was tired like a deadline running across a screen.
I felt like a bland grey
A sloth was awakening inside me.

Today
I feel hungry.
My stomach is feeling empty.
Today I am an empty bowl craving some food to fill me up.
If I were weather, I'd be a tsunami exploding
As I consumed the land around me.

Tonight
Tonight I will feel annoyed.
For when I get home tonight my brother will be there.
Instead, I shall annoy him and he will then cry at me.

Tomorrow
I feel like enslaving my brother and he shall work for me.
I'll then obliterate Trump's head and I'll be as happy as a dolphin.

Justin Lau
St Thomas More Catholic School, Bedford

YESTERDAY...

Yesterday
I felt excited, like a shining star and was as red as a robin flying all around me.

Today
Today I am feeling unhappy because I'm tired and I have to work most of the day at school like a cooker which then has a rest at night.

Tonight
I am doing my boring homework
And as I am writing I can taste the disgusting paper in my mouth.

Tomorrow
I am going to have a family meal in Spain and I am going to be happy and excited with the sky-blue sky around me
With the trees whistling and the hot air brushing over my shoulder.

Selina Borrelli
St Thomas More Catholic School, Bedford

YESTERDAY...

Yesterday
I was bored and bitter like a sour lemon with no hope of going home.

Today
I was a sleeping bag, so tired I cried.
Depressed and hot like a kettle.

Tonight
At least the game's on which makes me feel like I'm on top of the world.
There's also Fortnite which tastes like a delicious red and white candy cane.

Tomorrow
I want to have a lie in which will make me feel like a king.
I'll be on the plane to Italy with a Pepsi Max that isn't spilling.

Marco Catania
St Thomas More Catholic School, Bedford

YESTERDAY...

Yesterday
I was on top of cloud nine, dancing with joy like a ballerina wearing a purple tutu.
If I were an animal I would have been as happy as a warthog.

Today
I am a hippo, leader of the lake, doing this during lightning on a solar eclipse on a leap year.
And, in the distance, watching my fave team (Arsenal) thrash Manchester United 6-1!

Tomorrow
I will be a star performer in a roller hockey match, feeling bizarre.
A feeling so proud.
Just as if I'd won a gold medal in the Olympics.

Keira Stringer
St Thomas More Catholic School, Bedford

MIXED EMOTIONS

Today, I have been inspired
By the world around me
'Interesting' would be a word to describe it.

Yesterday, I was a rushing river
Flowing with ideas
Waiting to rupture with stories and songs
Silence filled my head as I swam deeper.

Tonight, I will dance across the lilypads
Time will go on forever and so will my feet
Syncronised stars skipping above my head
Until one day, there will be no more lilypads
I will swim in the black abyss.

Ciara Delaney
St Thomas More Catholic School, Bedford

FAR

Yesterday
I was a circle, dark blue in colour
Staring out into the sunset, silence overwhelmed me.
Today
Inside me it is cloudy
Yet there is sun hiding, waiting to be found.
Tomorrow
Music will ring through my ears
It will be sweet. Very sweet.
Tomorrow
I will go far, far away.
Disappear.
As if I am a bird in the night sky.

Naveen Prem
St Thomas More Catholic School, Bedford

I STAND

I stand overcome with cold, wet terror
Around me, the dark webbed sea
Pulses with fire and fury
Endless masses of veins forever
Throbbing and twisting
Folding over and flattening once more
Like melted wax and glass
Before thrusting itself against the cliffs
Bursting, shattering into the atmosphere
The spray hits me as sharp as sand
The wind ripples around me
And roars through the cliffs
That stand as fragile as china plates
Mangled chunks rising out of the bubbly spume
Like jagged teeth
What terror and fury is this?
That would smash people's skulls with its force
And leave the nation widowed and orphaned
Such power that is to be feared and envied by all man
Then behind me
Grandpa slips in the marshy ground
His hand on the fence does little to help
And his head replaces his heels
On the cold stony path
Suddenly my terror of the ocean
Compresses into a single drop,

On the ground at my feet
And with it the thought
That the only thing today
That threatened to harm a life
Was not the ringing winds
Or the mournful cliffs
Nor the writhing sea
But a stagnant pool of water
The size of my palm.

Natasha Lancaster (13)
The Cherwell School, Oxford

MY ANXIETY

I hear the music
Crash, bang, boom!
My head is dizzy,
My anxiety has started again.
The crowd roars as the next song starts,
All I see is a blur,
I walk over to the exit of the concert,
Constantly tripping over myself,
The pit in my stomach grows bigger and bigger.
I gag, I feel sick, and I vomit,
My friends are dancing happily,
Singing along joyfully,
I can't disturb them,
I have already ruined a concert before,
I can't do it again.
My headache is turning into a migraine,
I rush towards the toilet,
Too late.
I vomit again
The smell of trash food fills the air
I cry my eyes out,
Why did I convince myself to come here?
It always ends up the same way whenever I go to a concert.
I collapse on the floor...
I wake up,
I stumble back to my seat.

No one's there,
I have missed it,
A sigh of relief washes away, my anxiety like a wave
retreating back to the sea,
Why can I never enjoy anything?
This isn't fair.

Rita Iannacci (12)

The Cherwell School, Oxford

THE OUTLAW'S MEMOIR

Rotting in a musty cell,
He couldn't sing the Bible's verse,
For a single loaf of bread, his neighbour used to sell.
His hunger: a curse.
His state: from bad to worse.
Trapped in the chains which that curse quelled.

But one day:
Struggling, fighting, throwing,
The guard lay:
Sleeping, dying, groaning,
And the road of freedom stretched far away...

Rotting on the highway.
He's hidden in the thicket,
And draws his bow to hurt and maim.
Caught in his lawless net,
Encircled by his violent threats,
Each travelling million trapped in chains.

But one day:
Hacking, chopping, axing,
Only stumps remain:
Waning, dropping, taxing,
And the barren road of treason stretched far away...

Shot there in his own hall,
Caught in the act on that winding road.

His blackening head up on the wall.
Craven knights: they rode,
Innocence: a foreign code.
Betrayed by life, he took his fall.

Yet the crimes continue.

Leah Niamh Marshall (15)
The Cherwell School, Oxford

WHEN I SEE HIM

When I see him
My mind goes blank.
My heart beating so fast, so wild,
His eyes sparkle like stars in a midsummer's dream,
His smile brings life into me.
His voice, so soft, so pure.

When I see him
I can finally smile,
When I see him
I'm in a utopia,
Where the grass is green and the sky is blue,
Where we are together, away from all the darkness.
Where we are free and reminiscing about the times we shared together.
As we watch the sun go down
The trees turn brown,
We are old but still together.

When I see him
I feel numb.
When I see him
All my doubts dissipate.
When I see him
All my thoughts are free.
When I see him
I can breathe.

He is the ray of sunshine on me,
He gives me hope when I'm alone.
He gives me life when I'm with him.
When I see him,
When I hear his laughter,
Then, only then, I can finally smile,
When I see him.

Isha Dhanjal (13)
The Cherwell School, Oxford

2757

I have been thinking about this for a while now.
Why is that every man, woman and child never ask themselves how?
I mean why is it that everyone is made into a robot,
Getting fed the same thing again and again?

Wait, one more for safekeeping, again!
I always feel like a certain depression is creeping,
Always failing with no explanation,
For some reason, always questioning our own creation,
We are always never satisfied.

The economy's running low and no one really cares,
We always see people struggling to pay fares,
And the most shocking of all, questioning the system, well, no one dares,
But sadly this is common in 2757.

Oh yes, I forgot to mention, everyone has a damn gun,
My gun has never gotten shed blood.
But unlike others, I am not using it for fun,
Yes, that is right, this is my protest and for once it's good,
So savour it because as you are reading this, I am gone.

Sid Vaidya (12)
The Cherwell School, Oxford

ANIMAL FARM

Farmer Jones was a cruel man,
He hit the animals with a pan.
Along came Old Major and gave an idea,
But then died thinking about Pangea.

The animals thought of kicking out Jones,
Then they would be free with healthy bones.
In no time at all Jones was done,
So the animals just relaxed in the sun.

Napoleon and Snowball had a fight,
Then there was a vote to see who was right.
Snowball was gone and everyone was happy,
Soon Napoleon became surprisingly snappy.

The animals worked but Napoleon sat,
He wore clothes and wore a hat.
The animals were hurt, surprised and betrayed,
But they never complained as they were afraid.

Napoleon went against his own rules,
And the animals felt just like fools.
The pigs had turned into humans.
No one was trustworthy and this was proven.

Amina Zohra Riaz (13)
The Cherwell School, Oxford

THE SPELL NOBODY CAST

Sunlight filters through the cracks in the blinds,
Somebody sighs heavily.
Two girls are having a conversation across the room,
Entirely through eyebrow movements.
Someone drops a pencil,
Their chair scrapes as they push it back,
To reach the floor under the table.
Somebody coughs and two others echo it,
Silent laughter behind their hands.
Someone turns a page, sneaks a glance.
Somebody blows their nose noisily,
Several jump and stare.
A moment of perfect silence passes,
It might've been seconds or minutes.
The bell rings, jolting the room back to the land of the living.
Breaking the spell nobody cast.
The room is left empty when they've gone
And the silence stretches
In the still before fifth period.

Maya Legge (13)
The Cherwell School, Oxford

THE CLOUDS

The mist leisurely drifts around me,
Delicate feathers touch my face,
As they do, the air is filled with relief
And suddenly my troubles disappear.

The snow-like substance is calming,
There's a subtle breeze to guide me around,
I'm sinking into a pillow - soft like wool.

I unhurriedly drift off to sleep,
I am despondent because I know when I awaken
there won't be this candyfloss mattress beneath me
or this mountain of a sight.
In fact, I might never wake from this deep sleep.

As my sight fades I feel safe in the clouds.
My dreams are finally fading.
The sun dims into pure white - just like the clouds,
The clouds, I will always remember,
The clouds I will always adore.

Alice Wilkinson (11)
The Cherwell School, Oxford

FEELING LIKE YOU'RE UNDERWATER

You know that feeling, you feel when you're alone
And you feel like you've got nowhere else to go.
As if you're trapped inside a box,
And then your brain begins to clog.
Feeling as if everything has just crumbled.
The noises you hear come out mumbled and jumbled.
And no one listens if you try to shout out
Even if there are people about.
Your head then starts to feel so big.
All you want to do is dig.
But you can't because you feel so small.
Instead, you just roll into a ball.
By now you feel completely submerged,
There is no way you're going to re-emerge.
You feel like you're no longer a trotter,
This is the feeling like you're underwater.

Keeley Spencer (13)
The Cherwell School, Oxford

ALL ALONE

I sit there all alone,
I'm not sure where I am but I am definitely alone.
I'm not sure who I am,
I think my mind is grey, my heart is sad.
Something sits down next to me,
I think for a while, I know who it is,
It is a person just like me
But I don't want her to be one of them
So she can be an island I know very well,
I try and care but all she does is look away and stare.
She can hurt people in other ways
I won't mention any names.
I think her heart is sad and her mind is grey,
I hear these noises like scraping chairs,
They must be boats trying to stay afloat...
I wake up and it's all a dream
But she is sitting next to me...

Bella Whitty (12)
The Cherwell School, Oxford

FEAR

It was a gloomy night,
When the terrifying thunder pounded with an immersive roar.
The rain was falling powerfully and the wind was howling,
There was a house, not just any house; an ancient house,
With small, cracked windows smeared in green gunk.
A broken door.
The cedar shingles on the roof stood up like wonky teeth.
The house was surrounded by long, tall grass.
Hadn't been cut for years.
There was a man, solitary, living in here,
He leaves, a few hours later he reappears,
Exhausted, out of breath, confused and lonely,
Asking himself a question...
What's more terrifying?
Entering a home... or staying outside it?

Saira Ramzan (12)
The Cherwell School, Oxford

DOESN'T MATTER

Doesn't matter if you're someone's son or daughter
Doesn't matter if you don't think or look the same
Doesn't matter if you don't have a pretty face
Just as long as your heart's in the right place
Doesn't matter if you're young or old
Doesn't matter if you're dumb or bold
Doesn't matter if you don't have a pretty face
All that matters is your heart's in the right place
Doesn't matter if you're big or small
Doesn't matter if you're short or tall
Doesn't matter if you don't have a pretty face
Just as long as your heart's in the right place.

Isabella Smith (12)
The Cherwell School, Oxford

HER WORTH

You know my fears
You know my weakness
You know I'm not good enough
So why should I try and beat this?
You know my scars
And you know I'm falling apart.

You tell me to smile
And act like I'm fine
But deep down there's a battle I fight.
You tell me not to cry
Because that makes me weak
And I've already embarrassed myself
Three times this week.

You tell me I can't be happy
And that I'm worthless -
But guess what?
I have a purpose.
There's a fire that lit inside me today:
I remembered my worth
And that changed the whole game.

Poppy Felin (13)
The Cherwell School, Oxford

HONEYBEES

As I walk around my garden thinking,
My eyes fall upon the big miracle:
Honeybees sitting on nectar drinking,
So small and innocent yet visible.

Bees that are bright and sunny yellow,
Busy themselves all day with the big chore,
Making the honey makes them good fellows;
A sweet tasting morsel which they adore.

Bees that are frail and very powerless,
Do not welcome the invasions of space,
But their weapon to sting makes them fearless;
If you annoy them, they'll sting on your face.

Next time you see flowers, don't pick any:
You might get stung by bees - there are many!

Sameen Ahmed (12)
The Cherwell School, Oxford

THE LAST CHRISTMAS

As darkness falls on church and spire
A coldness fills the air
A robin sings in harmony
Its sound fills the square
But soon he will be gone to nest
To lay his tired head and rest
For coldness set in twig and branch
Has filled his tiny breast

He sleeps fitful and restless
As owls howl through the night
Waking cold and breathless
To the morning light
He starts to sing his plaintive song
But droop do his weary eyes
And breathing his last, he dies

And quiet is his funeral
As raised he is to Heaven
For he sang till the very end
Of Christmas, his old friend.

Sophie Meredith (13)
The Cherwell School, Oxford

HAPPINESS

You cannot buy happiness, 'cause happiness is free
You can't know, or can't guess, it's there for you and me
Just take a bite and see
That happiness is what you do
With something that is free.

Happiness is a cup of tea
Spending time together, just you and me
We talk and laugh,
It is sure to be love and affection.

Happiness is yours forever,
It's yours to keep,
Don't let anyone steal it from you,
It lives in you deep.

Cuddles and care could happily stay in forever,
Holding hands, we share a connection,
This is joy, this is bliss.

Christopher Sondai (12)
The Cherwell School, Oxford

MUM

We all need someone, on who we can depend
They are all very lucky, who have got their mums
When I grow older
I choose my own way
I realise what you give away
To be a mother and make the day
When I become sensible
And figure out the ups and downs of life
I witness the deductions mums make,
To be a mother and someone's wife
Here's to all of those mothers
What an amazing and fascinating woman you are,
You are not just a mother,
You are a shining star.
You've done so much for us and still do,
We just want to say, how much we love you.

Iqra Khan
The Cherwell School, Oxford

IN THE PARK

Birds tweeting everywhere,
People running here and there,
Blue skies, bright yellow sun,
No need to worry, all homework is done,
Clear lake, no ripples to be seen,
All bad weather has already been,
Children making daisy chains,
Swinging on swings without refrain,
Standing high are majestic trees,
Wearing a crown of dewy leaves,
Ducks waddling by the lake,
As people throw them bread, which they take,
All is well, all is well,
In the park, all is well.

Ottilie Carter (12)
The Cherwell School, Oxford

THE CROW

I was born in London
Inside a factory,
Where forever smog shall be.

I was sold as an infant
A murder of crows above did fly
One landed on my head and let out its cry.

And now I ride down the elevator
Dig, dig, mine, mine
And patiently, I wait for my time.

One day, I fell
Fell down the elevator shaft
Unsaved by the draught.

A crow landed on my head
It let out its mournful cry
To take me up to the next life.

Gabriel Wilkinson (14)
The Cherwell School, Oxford

FRIENDS

F ight for them, they would definitely do it for you.
R espect them, I'm sure they respect you.
I f. There are no 'ifs' about your friends, they just are your friends.
E xcited. If they are, be happy and excited for them too.
N ever betray them or be horrible to them, they are for life.
D efend them, stick up for one another.
S tay. You should stay loyal and respectful, peaceful and kind.

Chloe Enock (11)
The Cherwell School, Oxford

THE SKY IS ALIVE

The wind howled, swirled and danced around while arguing
with the clouds.
The clouds rained and hailed and threw lightning around.
The sunlight bounced harmlessly around, wanting to play
with the little toy planets.
The moon shouted at the sun, telling it to set while hugging
the stars close to its chest.
The stars snuggled up to the moon, they were waking but
the sun was still high.
The sky is alive, always has been and always will be.

Penelope Wilkinson (12)
The Cherwell School, Oxford

THE SCULPTED CONQUEROR

"He's coming..."

"I know,"

was all that was whispered
In the empty palace walls.

Away in the distance with his
Armed dogs he marched,
Steadfast and ready
To seize the throne and become
The Lord.

Behind the marble walls
The two stood together in unison
Facing the poor imitation of the Devil
Tet the crown feared not, since it was his creation.

Kirsten Kabanga Mpemba Nsendu
The Cherwell School, Oxford

TEMPORARILY FRIENDS

They're temporarily friends; it won't last long,
Each just waiting for someone more suitable to come along.

Using each other until they can escape their lives,
She's going to break out in unbearable hives.

Scratching and itching 'til she can breathe again,
When can she leave? When?

So the cycle repeats for the unsuited friends

Until they both meet their unfortunate ends.

Hannah Armour (17)
The Cherwell School, Oxford

SHE

No one could argue with her beauty and passion.
She was as lovely as a flower when in bloom,
Her eyes shining bright like sapphires.

Her lips were as red as a ruby.
The sea was as beautiful as her eyes.
Her lips were as lush as a strawberry.

She was as beautiful as the sunshine.
When she was beside me, I felt like flying.

Davina Ema Udoh (11)
The Cherwell School, Oxford

ODE TO MUSIC

Oh, wonderful melody!
Beautiful sound, lovely soothing rhythm.
Wonderful intertwining tones, handsome chords;
Wonderful composition.
Harmony, reminiscent of a sunrise.
Major chords, pulling happiness out of the saddest of people;
Deep minor chords, reminding you of the saddest of times.
A strong pulse you can feel inside you,
Like a heartbeat in your soul.
The sweet timbre of a violin, ringing in your ears,
Happy sounds of a flute, soaring into your feelings,
Melancholic cello, singing you a lullaby as you fall asleep,
Soft pizzicato bass, whispering secrets into your ears.
Why music, life's own sweet elixir,
Admirable melody, magnificent harmony,
Reassure me of the world's joy, eternally.

Elsa Rapisarda (15)
The Purcell School, Bushey

ODE TO FAMILY

My family is my world
Their unconditional love
Inspires me in life
To stay positive

When I'm feeling overwhelmed
Their support sustains me
Lifts my spirits high
To great horizons

They keep me grounded
And show me the way
To love others
And to love myself

Their encouragement is boundless
Through good times and bad
They see the best in me
No matter what

So many special memories
They give out so much
I am also there for them
Family. What else is there?

Ella Richardson (14)
The Purcell School, Bushey

YOUNG WRITERS INFORMATION

We hope you have enjoyed reading this book – and that you will continue to in the coming years.

If you're a young writer who enjoys reading and creative writing, or the parent of an enthusiastic poet or story writer, do visit our website **www.youngwriters.co.uk**. Here you will find free competitions, workshops and games, as well as recommended reads, a poetry glossary and our blog. There's lots to keep budding writers motivated to write!

If you would like to order further copies of this book, or any of our other titles, then please give us a call or visit **www.youngwriters.co.uk**.

Young Writers
Remus House
Coltsfoot Drive
Peterborough
PE2 9BF
(01733) 890066
info@youngwriters.co.uk

Join in the conversation!
Tips, news, giveaways and much more!

YoungWritersUK   @YoungWritersCW